MW00436343

Walking With God

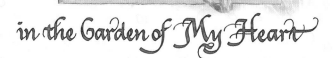

in the Garden of My Heart

Written and Illustrated by
AUDREY JEANNE ROBERTS

HARVEST HOUSE PUBLISHERS
EUGENE, OREGON

Walking with God in the Garden of My Heart

Text and Artwork Copyright © 2004 by Audrey Jeanne Roberts
Published by Harvest House Publishers
Eugene, OR 97402

ISBN 0-7369-1327-0

Design and production by Garborg Design Works, Minneapolis,
Minnesota

Printed in China.

04 05 06 07 08 09 10 11 12 13 / LP / 10 9 8 7 6 5 4 3 2 1

Contents

You are a garden locked up, my sister, my bride;
you are a spring enclosed...a garden fountain,
a well of flowing water streaming down from Lebanon...
Let my lover come into his garden and taste its choice fruits.

SONG OF SONGS 4:12,15-16

It Begins with a Plan

Did you know your heart is God's garden? He loves
making it a beautiful, fragrant, and fruitful place.
Amazingly, such work isn't drudgery to Him, but a task
that brings Him great joy and fulfillment.

Some of you are like a bare piece of ground, brand-
new to a spiritual walk of faith. Do you wonder where
to start and feel as though creating a beautiful garden is
an impossible and overwhelming process? Rest in this
thought—the Master Gardener doesn't expect the garden to make something of itself—that's His delightful
job! He expects to invest His time, strength, and all the
resources at His disposal to bring it to pass.

Some of you have had many years of relationship
with the Gardener but haven't quite been able to yield
the responsibility of tending your heart into His care.
Do you feel exhausted with the struggle? Has your
garden become overgrown and out of control? Does
it have rampant growth but no real maturity, sure
direction, or a cohesive plan? Do you look at its tangle
and wonder, "Where would God even begin?"

And there are some of you who have enjoyed many
years of the Master's care. You have discovered the joy of
meeting Him early in the morning, while the dew is still
on the roses. You have walked with Him in the cool of

the evening and enjoyed His fellowship, communion, and love. You have been incredibly changed—transformed from a wild tangle of wilderness into a beautiful secret garden created for His enjoyment and pleasure.

For each of you (and all of us in the many stages in between) God has a plan. His plan is unique and perfectly tailored to the specific challenges and opportunities your personality and life present Him. From the day God created your ground, He had a special plan for it. If you haven't yet entered into the process, it isn't hard to start—He is only awaiting your invitation to begin.

Lord, I want to give You the keys to my garden gate. I've kept it locked because, to be honest, I'm ashamed of my weedy garden. I want it to be so much more, but I don't have the strength, power, or ability to make it happen. It is so far from what I long for it to be. Please come into my heart and make it the beautiful secret garden You desire.

> *"For I know the plans I have for you," declares the Lord,*
> *"plans to prosper you and not to harm you,*
> *plans to give you hope and a future."*
>
> JEREMIAH 29:11

It Looks Worse, Not Better

You were looking through your garden magazines and savoring a restful vignette with a canopy of roses sheltering a table set with tea for two. You began daydreaming of the quiet days you would spend here in your garden with your dearest friend—when suddenly bulldozers showed up!

The process of transformation can be hard, much harder than you thought it would be. You didn't realize that the Gardener would have to tear down before He built new, or remove the mediocre to plant the spectacular. You knew He would have to build up the soil, but you didn't realize it would mean removing things you'd planted there. You feel as though you're going backward, not forward.

Perhaps the tiniest little thought is swirling around in the recesses of your mind, "I wish I had never started this. What was so bad about the way it was before? Perhaps I could have covered that ugly storage shed with some morning glory vines. Did it really need to be emptied and torn down?" You weren't prepared for the noise and find it unbearable. The work is messy, and everything looks disorganized and disheveled. Where's the beauty the Gardener promised you?

But trust Him, for He has a plan. He's clearing your land of its rubble and debris. He's delivering you from the dangers that were hiding behind the closed doors of the rusty old storage shed. He'll safely dispose of the containers of toxic waste that were also hidden there. He's prepared a place where they will never harm another soul and cannot come back to harm you, either. It is as far from here as the east is from the west and so deep that nothing thrown there can ever be brought up again—the totally environmentally safe Sea of His Forgiveness.

He's making you a clean, prepared place to create a masterpiece garden—a place more beautiful than you can imagine. One day soon you'll begin to see the progress that is being made. Until then, when you grow tired of the mess, ask Him to sit down with you, pull out the blueprints, and remind you once more about the beauty He has planned.

Lord, I didn't realize that the work You were going to do would be quite so extensive, noisy, and long! Thank You for taking away the brokenness of my previous life and the toxic waste I had stuffed away out of sight. Help me to hold on to Your promises and let You do every step necessary to make the garden of my heart into Your masterpiece.

Lord, make us mindful of
and blossom in these days to

He who owns a garden,
However small it be,
Whose hands have planted in it
Flower or Bush or Tree;
He who watches patiently
The growth from nurtured,
Who thrills a newly opened bloom
Is very close to God

KATHERINE EDELMAN

Adam was a gardener,
and God, who made
him, sees that half of
all good gardening is
done upon the knees.

RUDYARD KIPLING

he little things that grow
make the world beautiful for us.

W.E.B. DU BOIS

*As a father has compassion on his children, so the Lord
has compassion on those who fear him; for he knows how
we are formed, he remembers that we are dust.*

PSALM 103:13-14

Excellence, Not Perfection

As a classic, firstborn, overachiever perfectionist, one
of the earliest lessons I had to learn was perfection
simply isn't possible in the garden. I can try all I like,
but my garden never looks like the gardens I see in magazine spreads. I was frustrated until I read something
that set my heart free.

The story was written by a gardener whose yard had
recently been featured in a national magazine. She
revealed the behind-the-scenes manipulations required
to turn out those "perfect" garden shots.

She knew a year in advance the timing of the photo
shoot, so she planted anything and everything that
would bloom during that month. As planned, her garden was spectacular, but afterward there would be very
few flowers blooming in it for the rest of the year.

To shoot close-ups, the photographers meticulously
picked off every dead leaf from her potted plants and
picked blossoms from other parts of the garden, tuck-
ing them in to "enhance" the shots. Her potted plants
were moved all over the yard and even secretly tucked
into bare spots so they would photograph a little better.
To sum it up, she confessed that her garden bore about
as much relationship to achievable reality as a 5' 10",
120 pound runway model does to the average woman.

I'm glad that the Gardener of my heart is so much

more realistic and relaxed in His approach. He understands my frame. He knows there will be seasons of great beauty and abundant harvest and seasons where I am bare and dormant. He much prefers year-round excellence to spectacular short-lived perfection. He understands that when I am at my "peak glory" I'm only two weeks away from being bloomed out and bedraggled. He doesn't berate me for my natural limitations; He tucks new little plants in under the cover of the old so that I can continue bringing Him pleasure.

I still wrestle with perfectionism. I easily panic when a weed sprouts up in my heart or I feel I failed to perform up to my capabilities. I don't allow for the frailty that is my human nature—but my Father the Gardener does. He understands me, He loves me, and He thinks I'm pretty special—dead leaves and all.

Lord, I have such a hard time with having unrealistic expectations and then feeling like a failure. Help me to understand who I am, how You made me, and what Your expectations are of me. Help me to quit comparing myself to others and strive for excellence—not perfection.

Glorious Compost

Nowhere on the face of the earth do I feel closer to
God than I do when turning my compost pile. I
absolutely love composting. I often go quite a long time
between batches while I'm gathering materials, but once
I've started I'm incredibly compulsive about tending my
pile. Every single day I take a temperature reading to see
how it's progressing. You should see my face light up
when it's reached 160 degrees and those nasty little
weed seeds are cooking.

Composting is a wonderful picture of the process
of redemption. The Master Gardener can take almost
anything that is dead and useless and make from it a
life-nourishing resource. He uses the very branches He
has pruned from us to fuel our future fruitfulness. Even
immature weeds and dead plants can be transformed
from life-sappers to life-givers.

The only difference between wasteful trash that
clutters up a garden and useful compost that brings it
vitality and life is what we choose to do with it. If we're
ashamed of our past disobediences or mistakes and
shove them into an unused portion of the garden, they
will take a very long time to decompose and look quite

ugly until they do. Shame will grow in our hearts, and every time we enter that part of the garden, we'll have the desire to hide from the Gardener, not run toward Him.

However, if we fearlessly and humbly hand our mistakes, failures, and overgrowth to the Gardener, asking Him to redeem them, He does so with great delight. While He will instruct us, He never shames or condemns us. He is our redeemer, and He not only has the power to bring good out of evil, He loves doing it!

Of course, not everything we give Him is fit for the compost pile. Insidious weeds and diseased plants need to be firmly cast away so that they do not spread their destruction throughout the garden. He discerns perfectly what can and can't be redeemed. Our job is simply to give it all to Him and let Him decide.

He teaches us from our mistakes so that we may grow and in turn teach others. He is capable of transforming devastating events from our past into beauty and fruitfulness today. Out of our very weakness and frailty He delights in creating health, vitality, and strength.

Lord, when I make a mistake, disobey You, or have just been pruned after trying to grow in my own strength, I want to run and hide the evidence in the back corner of my garden. Help me to give everything to You so that You can redeem it and show me how much You love bringing forth new life out of disaster and disappointment.

I am the true vine, and my Father is the gardener...
I am the vine; you are the branches. If a man remains
in me and I in him, he will bear much fruit.

JOHN 15:1,5

The Joyful Reward of Growth

Throughout the Word, God is called our "Husbandman," "the Vinedresser," and "the Gardener." A husbandman was one who tended to land, orchards, and vineyards, and whose responsibility it was to produce a fruitful crop. Interestingly, though I've searched the Word carefully, I can't find a verse wherein the Lord is called "the Housekeeper of our Souls."

I have some rather unusual quirks that have caused me to search my heart very closely, examining both my character and my motivation. You see, I'm frequently guilty of walking past loads of laundry and dishes for a day or two before I'll buckle down and attend to them (assuming my darling husband hasn't quietly dispatched them before I can get around to it!).

On the other hand, I can't tolerate my lawn not being neatly mowed or oak leaves piling up on the brick patio. I hate seeing weeds crowd out the plants in my garden, and it's "shear" joy to take the hedge trimmer to the various topiaries I have growing about my landscape.

I'm coming to understand why I'm more motivated to work in the garden than in my house. In my garden

things grow and get better. The work I do today will still be visible next week—and even show an increase. Yet after hours spent cleaning my house, I'm barely minutes away from it degenerating into chaos once again.

Like my Father the Gardener, I love growth. It's an amazing concept. Insignificant things like seeds and acorns with time and care can become beautiful flowers or mighty sheltering trees. When I come home from another of my frequent road trips, I'm drawn to measure every bit of growth that occurred while I was away. I meander through the paths and marvel at the roses now blooming or the magic lilies sprouting out of nowhere to brighten the garden in the hottest part of the summer. It's rewarding to see so much change happen in just a few weeks.

I realize that my picture of the Lord has sometimes been more akin to a "Housekeeping Nazi" who chases me around the house with a wooden spoon, irritated at the mess I've made of things! But in reality He's a tender husbandman who nurtures and creates the very best conditions for me to grow and then stands back and admires my beauty.

Lord, sometimes my picture of You is closer to the
"Housekeeping Nazi" than the tender Gardener.
Please change that picture in my heart and mind
so that I can begin to sense Your delight in nurturing
and caring for me, and then standing back to reap
the joyful rewards of watching me grow.

I do not think I have ever seen anything more beautiful than the bluebell I have been looking at. I know the beauty of our Lord by it.

GERARD MANLEY HOPKINS

In my garden there is a large place for sentiment thoughts and dreams. The thoughts grow as free.

We can complain because
rose bushes have thorns,
or rejoice because
thorn bushes have roses.

ABRAHAM LINCOLN

My garden of flowers is also my garden of
 s the flowers, and the dreams are as beautiful.

ABRAM L. URBAN

The Transformation of a Princess

I really wish you could have seen me yesterday in all my glory. It's my daughter Jacqui's job to run the water in our grove, but she's away for the summer. My husband would love to have taken over the task, but he's up to his ears in crucial responsibilities elsewhere. So, even though the "princess" is abysmal at all things mechanical or operational, summer's here, the orange trees are withering in the heat, and no attendants are available to accomplish the task. I had to tackle the watering alone.

By the end of the afternoon I was soaked to the skin, my jeans had mud and weed stains from mid-thigh to mid-calf, and my hair looked as though I had been through a tornado (twigs and orange leaves were mixed attractively throughout the knots). The lovely T-shirt I was wearing had been covered with mud splashes and dandelion seeds, but you could still read the inscription, which began "Lord, bless this land…"

I had, however, managed to repair most of the shattered hose lines and sprinkler sleds that I had destroyed while working another day with my "weed whacker on steroids." I also made certain each sprinkler was operating appropriately.

When snails, slugs, ants, or other creepy crawly things need water, they climb into sprinkler hoses to find it. If a sprinkler isn't working, you have to pull it apart and try to get rid of anything that's stuck inside. The first resort is to tap it on a tree or blow hard from the outside of the sprinkler head, trying to dislodge the blockage. The last resort is to put the thing in your mouth and give it a hard suck. I did that yesterday and managed to suck out a slug. UUUUUGGGGHHH!

If God had told "Princess Audrey" when she was 21 and headed on a career track that He was taking her on an exciting journey that would lead to yesterday's adventure, do you think she would have signed up?

God's a little smarter than that. He starts us on the path little by little. I went from tending some potted plants on my condo balcony and then struggling with a 50 x 100 city lot for 20 years to becoming pretty much fully responsible for one acre of landscaping and partially responsible for four acres of oranges. At the beginning of my journey I never would have believed I would either be capable of the task or would desire to fulfill it.

Day by day God is preparing you for a little more difficult assignment. The preparation is often hard and the assignment sometimes harder than you would have signed up for or believed you were capable of accomplishing, but your Father the Gardener knows perfectly well that you'll ultimately find great satisfaction and peace in it. So give in and let Him take you where He will, and you'll discover the amazing destiny He has for your life.

Lord, I couldn't have imagined a few years ago where You would have me today—and I'm sure I can't even come close to imagining where You'll have me in a decade. Please keep me moving on the path to fulfilling the destiny You have for my life, especially on those days when I want to sit down and refuse to move any farther!

Each one should use whatever gift he has received to serve others,
faithfully administering God's grace in its various forms.
I PETER 4:10

Winged Jewels

Shrimp plants are funny-looking things. Their blossoms are peachy coral velvet with small white tidbits coming out of their centers. Each segment of the flower nests in the one above it, forming the distinctive blossom from which the plant derives its common name.

I grow nostalgic when I see them and think back to my childhood days. Every home we lived in had one. My mother planted them for the hummingbirds they attracted.

Often she would call me over to the plate glass window that overlooked her shade garden, and we would watch the hummingbirds dart to and fro…hovering at this blossom and then that one until they had drunk their fill. We would quietly, reverently exclaim over the beautiful ruby red throats and the iridescent sheen of these tiny birds, being careful to hold very, very still so that we wouldn't chase the winged jewels away.

A well-thought-out garden has many plants like the shrimp plant—they're supporting cast members, not superstars. Some are plants that feed and attract birds and butterflies, some grow and bloom in the deepest, darkest shade, and others have elegant, neutral foliage

which functions as a backdrop highlighting the more spectacular blossoms of its neighbors. Each is chosen to serve a useful and important purpose.

The Lord tucks some of these plants in my garden as well—plants like "humility," "self-sacrifice," "hospitality," and "gentleness." You have to look pretty hard to pick them out because they're rather drab and ordinary in appearance. They don't tend to draw attention to themselves. They like it best when others are in the spotlight, yet it is their quietly rendered service that makes the garden come vibrantly alive with beauty.

Lord, I know You've wanted to plant these traits
in my heart for quite a while, but I've left them over
in the corner of the garden because they weren't
as pretty and spectacular as I'd like. Please,
plant them now, Lord, and let me enjoy the beautiful
"winged jewels" they will begin to attract!

No branch can bear fruit by itself; it must remain in the vine.
Neither can you bear fruit unless you remain in me.

JOHN 15:4

The Supporting Branches

My husband and I wanted to build a large garage and workshop on our property, but to do so we had to remove 35 orange trees. During the process my husband found a worker halfway through cutting down an extra tree and hurriedly stopped him. It was pretty well mangled, but it would survive.

A year or so later I was walking through the grove thinking about my first husband's death. He had lost a battle with cancer, and I had gone through a potentially devastating season in my life—financially, emotionally, and spiritually. Yet through it all God's love and grace had filled my heart and soul. I hadn't always felt His presence, but I knew He was there the whole time. Much of His love was experienced through the tender care of my church family and my lifelong friends.

Right at this point in my musings, I came to the half-cut-down orange tree. Where the branches had been destroyed, new growth was springing up to fill in. I smiled as I thought about new life for old, and then I noticed something very, very unusual about the tree.

There was the stump of a large branch cut off from the trunk, yet about a foot higher this same branch continued on—apparently suspended in midair. Following the branch upward I expected to see dead leaves, but amazingly the branch was not only very much alive—it was the most fruitful branch on the tree! How could this be when it had been severed from the trunk?

Looking more closely, I discovered the branch had lain so heavily against two other nearby branches that it had grafted itself into them and they had become one. When the branch was cut off, it drew its sustenance and strength from the other branches. It had survived and even thrived because it had become one with the other two branches.

Those two branches speak to my heart of the church family and our relationship with the Lord. As we grow closer to each of them, we are often sustained by their nurture and love. Are you grafted in to the body of Christ? Is your heart bonded to those who also love Him? Are you abiding in Christ Himself and His love? The time to develop these relationships is now—before times of trouble come. You may find, just as I did, that the love of Jesus and His people has the power to sustain you and make you more fruitful than you can imagine.

Lord, help me to develop the relationships around me.
Let my life be made strong and secure in the good times
so that if tough times come I have the resources to survive.
Make me strong enough to be leaned upon and humble
enough to lean upon others when I need to.

*Take my yoke upon you and learn from me, for I am
gentle and humble in heart, and you will find rest
for your souls. For my yoke is easy and my burden is light.*

MATTHEW 11:29-30

Overloaded with Fruit

I pulled around the driveway in front of our house and
noticed a very large apricot branch blocking my way.
The tree had split into three parts, the largest two of
which were lying across the road. The trunk was twisted
and torn into shreds. I got out of the car so I could
look closely to check for any apparent pest infestation
or disease, but found none. It was clear that the apricot
tree was destroyed solely by the weight of its own fruitfulness.

I felt both devastated and guilty. I've lived here four
years and intended to prune the tree back each year, but
I didn't quite know how or when to do it. I was always
planning to learn about it, but my schedule was a little
too busy to fit it in. My inexperience and inattentive-
ness may have cost this tree its life.

Pruning is a vital protection to a fruit tree. Setting
boundaries for its growth allows it to safely put all of
its energy into the production of fruit. It makes the
process a restful one—and an easy burden for the tree.

A tree that is allowed to grow this way and that year
after year becomes weak and overextended. If my tree
had been routinely trimmed, it would have produced a
greater quantity of sweet, large fruit, and it would have
done so for many more years. Now I may have no other
choice than to cut it down to the ground.

Our lives can easily become like that apricot tree. Most of us have the bad habit of adding task after task, activity after activity, and not stopping to think about limits. We resist the trimming of our branches into safe boundaries that will keep us producing sweet fruit for many years to come.

Unlike a tree that has no say in whether or not it will be pruned, we can either submit to God's work in our life or run from it. When we are afraid to stand still while He prunes us, we need to remember a short burst of incredible fruitfulness will never come close to equaling the yield of a well-balanced, consistent, long-lived effort. The Lord wants us to have restful, fruitful lives that are filled with joy and not weighted down with heavy burdens that have the potential of destroying us.

Lord, I have to confess I don't like to see You headed
my way with Your pruning saw in Your hands!
I often can't discern between my branches to know
which to keep and which must go. Please show
me what activities, commitments, and responsibilities
should be retained and which need to be removed.
Give me the courage to trust You and hold still
no matter how much I want to run away.

A gardener learns more in the

*Sweet flowers are
slow and weeds
make haste.*

WILLIAM SHAKESPEARE

*More grows in
the garden than the
gardener sows.*

OLD SPANISH PROVERB

mistakes than in the successes.

BARBARA BORLAND

Each garden has its own surprise.
SUSAN ALLEN TOTH

*No discipline seems pleasant at the time, but painful.
Later on, however, it produces a harvest of righteousness
and peace for those who have been trained by it.*

HEBREWS 12:11

The Process of Pruning

Personally, I've always hated the idea of entering into
a season of pruning. For most of my Christian
walk, when I thought about pruning, I preferred to
envision the Gardener picking up His shears and gently
comforting me. Surely He would do His work quickly,
doing the least amount of pruning necessary so that I
could keep on growing. He would be anxious to move
on to other, more pleasant tasks. Then I moved to my
farm…

Everywhere I looked there were things growing on
top of things, tangled undergrowth, and out-of-control
plants seeking to invade and take over the garden. I had
trees with sucker growth as big as full-size trees and
vines with three-inch diameter stems that had spread up
and into the ancient oak trees.

An interesting thing began to
happen in my heart. I awoke each
day, dressed in my gardening
clothes, and put my pruning
shears into my pocket.
"Have pruning shears,
will travel," became
my motto. Every day
I entered the garden

with one joyful purpose: to free the garden from the tyranny of self-rule.

I found I was not at all timid or apologetic but went forward with a vengeance. I was on a mission. What could I trim back or cut down? What could I prune into a more pleasing shape or balanced size? From my perspective pruning was a joyful process, for I could envision the results as I worked.

It was then that I realized God probably looked at my life a lot like I was looking at my garden. He wasn't sorry that He was going to prune me back…He was joyful! He saw the end result from the very start and didn't mourn. He rejoiced instead at the new growth cutting back would produce. He saw the shape and place He had planned for every bush, tree, and vine and how they would work beautifully together. He also knew how dangerous weakened branches could be in a storm.

The Lord changed the attitude of my heart, and He longs to change yours as well. Will you invite Him into your garden with pruning shears in hand?

Lord, I have a hard time being excited by
the thought of being pruned back. I confess that
I rather like "self-rule" and don't actually look forward
to having a Master taking care of me. There are
times I'd even like to hide Your pruning shears
and delay the inevitable. Please change my heart
and help me to see this process the way You see it.

A Snip at a Time

Once I'd overcome my fear of God's pruning, I
began to realize pruning is a continual process. I'd
always imagined it might have to occur every few years,
maybe less if I was a "good" Christian girl. It was
something to be endured and then put behind me as I
went on to better things. But then I began to notice
almost every time my Father came to tend my garden,
He brought his pruning shears with Him.

At first He was making large, drastic cuts. It seemed
every time He entered the garden, wheelbarrow loads
left it. At first I fretted over every missing branch, but
over time I began to enjoy the extra dappled sunlight
His ministrations had brought in. I even discovered
plants beginning to bloom that had previously been
hindered by the darkness.

Soon I realized my life was more manageable under
His control. I also discovered that pruning was much
easier when it happened during our daily walks in the
garden…a gentle clip here, a shaping there, and perhaps
a little thinning out of some branches to bring in more
light. I began to receive this kind of attention as part of
His loving care for me, and it became a very important
part of our intimate communion together.

Just like my wild garden, the garden of my heart
had lived under the tyranny of self-rule. The strongest
characteristics of my nature had taken over and crowded

out everything else.
My Father the
Gardener taught
me they must
be brought into
balance in order
to nurture lesser
characteristics that were
of great value to Him. The

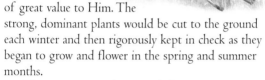

strong, dominant plants would be cut to the ground
each winter and then rigorously kept in check as they
began to grow and flower in the spring and summer
months.

The more rare and treasured characteristics were
often quite frail and sensitive, requiring almost no
pruning at all. He understood each and began to bring
great variety into what had once been a very lackluster
landscape.

Having a loving Master makes us truly free! We
became more, not less. Stronger, not weaker. "For whoever wants to save his life will lose it, but whoever loses
his life for me will save it" (Luke 9:24). I cannot imagine anywhere else on earth the truth of that statement
is more clearly seen than in the garden.

Lord, I have some pretty dominant character traits.
Perhaps they've taken over my garden and I don't
even know what else You might have under them
just waiting to come into the light. Please cut them
back so that You can bring more variety and beauty
into the garden of my heart.

Anyone can count the number of seeds in an apple,

Earth's crammed
with heaven and
every common bush
afire with God:
But only he who sees
takes off his shoes.

ELIZABETH BARRET BROWNING

I think that if ever a mortal heard the voice of

but only God can count the number of apples in a seed.

ROBERT H. SCHULLER

God it would be in a garden at the cool of the day.

F. FRANKFORT MOORE

Those who hope in the Lord will renew their strength.
They will soar on wings like eagles, they will run
and not grow weary, they will walk and not be faint.

ISAIAH 40:31

The Other Side
of the Storm

My sister Brenda lives on the island of Kauai, which was profoundly devastated in September 1992 by a hurricane named Iniki. With wind gusts up to 175 mph, it wreaked incredible havoc on the island's buildings, businesses, and gardens. Many homes and their entire contents were lost, but because of the storm, the people gained a greater appreciation for each other and for life itself.

One of the oddities I remember most about the storm was its impact on the vegetation—for Kauai is known as "The Garden Isle." Trees a hundred years old and more were uprooted, and those that remained were shattered and broken. Virtually every leaf on the entire island was torn off, leaving an appearance of total death and destruction—yet in a matter of weeks the island began to spring to life again.

God created in nature an amazingly high-speed "recovery mode." The storm breaks and destroys, but it also begins a powerful process of renewal and regeneration. The plants and fruit trees on Kauai began blooming out of season, and some even produced two crops in the next year. The island would never be exactly the same again, but it developed an entirely new growth and beauty in response to the loss of the old.

Farmers use this principle in managing many types of fruit trees. Orange trees have a life expectancy of about 80-85 years, but they begin to dramatically decrease in fruitfulness at midlife. They can be allowed to simply wither away a little more each year, or they can be radically cut back to nothing more than about four feet of trunk. Amazingly, this trauma will renew their youth, causing them to produce a greater crop for their remaining years.

Powerful storms sometimes have devastating impacts on the landscape of our lives. They can steal away one we love or produce illness or the loss of a career—yet God can also use the storm as His vehicle to renew our strength and youth. That which was meant to destroy can unleash a powerful process of recovery that will lead to increased fruitfulness—as long as we don't give up and quit growing.

It certainly isn't easy to survey the changed landscape of your life after a storm. It's even harder to ask God to give you hope and a new vision for the uncertain future that lies ahead. It's difficult to hand over the broken and battered pieces of the old, but be assured that He has amazing power to utilize even the worst storm to bring new beauty and fruitfulness to your life.

Father, I hate the unexpected devastating storms of life that sometimes come my way. Help me to face them with courage and recover from them by not asking, "Why, God, why?" but "What can You accomplish in my heart as You cause me to grow through the pain of this loss?" Make what Satan meant for evil bring forth a double crop of good.

*The God of all grace, who called you to his eternal
glory in Christ, after you have suffered a little while,
will himself restore you and make you strong, firm and steadfast.*

1 PETER 5:10

A Living Picture of Grace

The weekend after I discovered my apricot tree shattered into pieces on my driveway, my husband stood with chainsaw in hand preparing to cut the remains of the tree down. Everything I knew about fruit trees told me it would be impossible to save this one. The remaining trunk had a split running almost a foot down its center, and 18 inches of the core was fully exposed. If shock hadn't already killed the tree, pests and disease were sure to follow and finish the job.

As Steve prepared to start his chainsaw, a still small voice spoke to my heart. "Wait and watch what will happen next. Let this story unfold all the way to its end." I began to sense there would be something more to learn as I watched God at work.

Within weeks a few new shoots valiantly struggled to emerge before shriveling away as the cold of winter began to set in. The bareness of the dormant season left the ugly, twisted, scarred trunk nakedly exposed. All we could do was wait for spring's verdict—would our tree live or die?

As spring approached I was determined to learn from my mistakes. I thoroughly researched pruning techniques, and we cut back what remained of the damaged tree. We shaped it to grow into a safe size and direction.

As the weather began to warm, the tree sprang to life

with great vigor. In fact, I had to remove 50 percent of the new growth to make certain it was balanced with an open, airy shape. It is only one-third the size of its twin, yet amazingly it will produce some fruit this year, and within another year it will probably be fully restored.

As much as this surprised me, there was yet another surprise in store for me. Every year more fruit is left on the ground than we harvest, so the seeds pile up and eventually decay. This year, because of our pruning, more sunlight was able to reach the ground and a dozen of them have grown into new seedlings that we're going to be able to give away or transplant.

Every time I see my apricot tree I marvel at the awesome grace of God. My life, like my tree's, has been miraculously kept from certain death in spite of my own foolish decisions and mistakes. The Lord's grace prevented devastating consequences from destroying me—even though they should have. And in the very shadow destruction cast, He caused seeds of blessing to spring to life. What amazing, overwhelming, incredible grace.

Lord, help me recognize the evidence of Your grace in my life. Thank You that You have never given me what I deserve. Instead, You have showered me with Your incredible protection, kindness, and love. Even though my trunk's a little gnarled and I'm a wee bit warped, help me keep reaching for the sunshine so I might produce a harvest of fruitfulness for You.

U.G.O.

One morning while tending to my plants on our front deck, I noticed a really interesting specimen. I'd never seen anything quite like it before. I was fairly certain it was some type of a sunflower. Many farms in our community grow commercial flowers, and sunflowers are common among them. Perhaps the crows that nested in our oak trees had brought it in.

We nicknamed it our "U.G.O." for "Unidentified Growing Object." My family watched it with fascination. Its stalk was strong and had a mixture of a bright fuchsia-purple striped with green. The leaves were large and very similar to those of a sunflower. Week after week it grew. Finally, it had soared to over 15 feet tall! We waited excitedly for what we knew was going to be a truly spectacular flowering.

Spectacular? When it finally bloomed, it sputtered out tiny, absolutely ugly stinky little "flowers." We laughed so hard when we realized we'd just grown the most enormous weed any of us had ever seen!

Had I the wisdom and experience of the Master Gardener, I would have known right from the start that no matter how pretty the plant appeared, it would never produce anything worthwhile. How sad I was the day I ripped it up. In its place was left a large messy hole, and all of the plants that surrounded it had become weak and sickly.

Pride and self-confidence can be like that U.G.O.,
looking impressive to the world and those around us.
They grow spectacularly large and appear lovely to the
eye, but the end result is that no good thing will ever
come from them. Only the Lord knows right from the
start what will be fruitful in our lives and what is nothing but a seductive and destructive weed.

Seeds of God's nature produce a peaceable harvest
of righteousness; seeds of our flesh do not. How can
we know the difference? I like to look in God's gardening guide—His Word. It's like a comprehensive gardening book that shows every weed and fruitful plant in
various stages of growth. If I study it well, and look
into the garden of my heart, I can learn from the
Gardener's wisdom
and experience. I
can recognize the
shape and form
of the weeds
while they are
still quite small
and easily pull
them out.

Please come and tend my garden. Pull out the weeds—
both those I find attractive and full of promise
as well as those I recognize and dislike. Lord, I don't
have much experience in knowing which seed will
produce good fruit in my life. Help me learn to recognize
weeds when they are small and easily removed
so Your good seed can flourish in my heart.

God almighty first planted a garden.
And indeed, it is the purest of human pleasures.

FRANCIS BACON

Sometimes the tiniest

Kiss of the sun for pardon,
Song of the birds for mirth,
You're closer to God's heart in a garden
Than any place else on earth.

DOROTHY FRANCES GURNEY

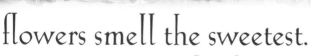

flowers smell the sweetest.

EMILIE BARNES

Overgrown with Mint

I once had a flowerbed in a prime location that was overrun with mint, every gardener's worst nightmare. I knew it would take a great deal of time and work to reclaim the bed.

I carefully dug it out and let the ground lay fallow. At first every few weeks I would notice little pieces of mint reaching for the sun. After faithfully removing them, I would return to watching. Little by little I gained the upper hand, and finally six months had gone by with no evidence of life. After a full 18 months I felt it was safe to begin planting flowers where the mint had once reigned.

After the long battle, I found I had an extra special delight in this garden. This was the first time in my life I hadn't rushed the process, so I was overjoyed when the time finally came to replant it! Three new roses and various perennials beautifully filled out the 25' x 8' border.

The Master Gardener knows the difference between common and insidious weeds that live in our hearts. The common weeds are easily dealt with, and sometimes it's as though He miraculously eliminates them with no effort on our part. But the tougher, insidious ones like gossiping, lying, anger, impatience, and covetousness don't go quite so quickly or easily.

Like mint, it takes the Gardener a great deal of time and effort to eradicate them, but He diligently perseveres. He ruthlessly seeks out every tiny vestige remaining in our hearts, knowing how easily these things can come back into domination.

Often when He's working on an overrun section in the garden of my heart, I want to hang my head in shame and quit. But always His gentle voice reassures me He isn't disappointed or surprised that weeds are still lurking there. Then He chuckles and reminds me that a garden can't weed itself! My works can't free me—only His strength and diligence can.

One day, He assures me, He will replant this patch of ground and take great joy and pleasure in it. Where "lying" once reigned, "love-of-the-truth" will grow. It will be paired with "honor," "integrity," and "courage." He will finish by planting the thick groundcover of "purity of speech" to ensure that it will never again be overtaken by weeds. He alone can transform that patch of weedy-weakness into a stronghold of strength and beauty.

Lord, sometimes I become discouraged because of these sins that keep rising up from deep within the recesses of my heart. I can't seem to gain victory over them. Please come and work this part of my garden. Dig them out from the root up and help me to be patient as You complete the process. Fulfill my joy and Yours as together we see what You will one day plant in their place.

We all, with open face beholding as in a glass the glory
of the Lord, are changed into the same image
from glory to glory, even as by the Spirit of the Lord.

2 CORINTHIANS 3:18 KJV

The Glory of the Garden

Wouldn't it be silly to look at a garden and exclaim, "See how beautiful the garden has made itself!" We understand that every great garden has a master whose guidance, plans, and diligent efforts have brought it to peak glory. The garden's glory belongs to its keeper.

The gardener's challenges come from the elements, the land itself, and destructive pests and diseases. He's usually not fighting the will of the plants he is caring for. His trees can't get up and run away when he heads in their direction with pruning shears in hand. An overgrown clump of perennials won't cry out in protest if he begins dividing it with his shovel. It doesn't know he is planning for its renewal by dividing it and transplanting some portions to another part of the garden. A real-life garden is the passive recipient of its master's care.

However, the Master Gardener's very first challenge in our hearts is to overcome our unwillingness to be tended! How often have we run away when He tried to reduce our activity load by pruning away opportunities that will not bring sweet, large fruit? We've refused to consider that He may wish to bring change in our lives as He plans to move us to another community or into a different place of work or ministry. We've jealously guarded relationships that have grown quite close but, like overgrown perennial beds, need to be thinned or they will no longer flower.

How well do you allow the Master Gardener to tend your garden? Is it your natural inclination to run from the pain of the moment and not see the reward that enduring His tending will produce? Sometimes I have a hard time matching my challenging experiences with the fruit they produced a year or two later. Do you have a hard time with that too? He can help each of us to understand and even enjoy the process of producing fruitfulness in our lives. All we have to do is ask Him.

Lord, help me to hold still and resist the urge to run
away when I sense You are at work in my heart.
Help me understand the fruitful purposes that often
attend the painful seasons of pruning in my life.
Give me understanding of Your ways. Teach me
to learn from past events so I might grow—and then
give me the ability to use that understanding to see
ahead with eyes of faith and courage.

I always pray with joy...being confident of this, that he who began a good work in you will carry it on to completion until the day of Christ Jesus.

PHILIPPIANS 1:4-6

Three Weeks Away from Ruin

Two of my favorite magazines are *The English Home* and *The English Garden*. I look through them from cover to cover to find gardening ideas or inspiration for my painting. In these wonderful publications you commonly see two distinct garden styles, and I love them both. There's the wild, rambunctious, spilling-over-the-top-of-everything cottage garden, and its antithesis, the intricately manicured, ordered, and clipped formal garden.

My own garden (like its master!) leans much more towards the wild and out-of-control side. You see, as much as I love formal gardens, the reality is I will never have the discipline, diligence, or the time required to be the master of a formal garden.

Several stories have profiled once-magnificent estate properties that were restored to their former glory by new owners—the process often taking decades to complete. Yet, even after a finished restoration, the most magnificent gardens are still only three weeks away from potential ruin.

Why? Because grand gardens actually require more care, not less; and that care must be of the highest caliber. Specialized knowledge of rare trees and plants, understanding each plant's blooming season, and how to keep a garden at exhibition level all year long are just the starting points.

An estate property almost always has a large greenhouse facility where the greatest amount of work is done behind the scenes, away from the public's view. New growth gets its start in this hidden place and is carefully nurtured and prepared ahead of time so that when its season arrives, it's ready to be released onto center stage in the public garden.

If gardens could talk, could you imagine the Biltmore estate's saying, "Thanks, guys, we'll take it from here"? Pretty silly—yet that's the attitude I can easily adopt when I've grown a little and my life starts flourishing. I constantly remind myself that no matter how much I learn or how mature I may become, I'm just like one of those gardens—potentially only three weeks away from ruin. Whether I'm leading a women's Bible study, taking time off to raise my family, or speaking to women's groups and writing books—I'm desperately in need of the wise care of a seasoned Master if I want to continue to grow and flourish.

Lord, I surely don't feel much like a magnificent garden, but You think I am. Remind me as I grow in You that I will need more daily maintenance, not less. Keep planting new things in the greenhouse of our quiet time so they can increase in strength until it's their time to be put on public display.

The Lord will
guide you always;
he will satisfy
your needs in
a sun-scorched
land and will
strengthen your
frame. You will be
like a well-watered
garden, like a
spring whose
waters never fail.

ISAIAH 58:11